The Great Depression

American history, Volume 6

Michael Johnson

Published by Harmony House Publishing, 2024.

THE GREAT DEPRESSION

First edition. March 29, 2024.

Copyright © 2024 Michael Johnson.

ISBN: 979-8224405022

Written by Michael Johnson.

Table of Contents

"To those who weathered the storm of the Great Depression, and to the generations who carry its legacy forward, this book is dedicated. In honor of the resilience, perseverance, and enduring spirit of the American people during one of the nation's darkest hours. May their stories of hardship and hope serve as a guiding light for us all, inspiring empathy, compassion, and a commitment to building a more just and equitable society."

Chapter 1: Setting the Stage

Introduction to the Economic Boom of the 1920s

The 1920s in America were characterized by rapid economic growth, technological advancement, and cultural change. Following the end of World War I, the United States experienced a period of prosperity unlike any seen before. This era, often referred to as the "Roaring Twenties," was marked by a surge in consumerism, industrial expansion, and stock market speculation.

The end of World War I brought about a period of optimism and confidence in the American economy. The nation had emerged from the war as a global superpower, with its industrial capacity largely intact. The demand for American goods soared both domestically and internationally, fueling an economic boom that would define the decade.

One of the key drivers of the economic growth during the 1920s was the rise of mass production and assembly line techniques pioneered by companies such as Ford Motor Company. These innovations led to increased efficiency and lower production costs, making consumer goods more affordable to the average American. The automobile industry, in particular, experienced exponential growth, revolutionizing transportation and stimulating related industries such as steel, rubber, and oil.

Technological advancements also played a significant role in shaping the economic landscape of the 1920s. The widespread adoption of electricity, telephones, and radio transformed both urban and rural life, facilitating communication, entertainment, and commerce on an unprecedented scale. The proliferation of new consumer products and conveniences contributed to a culture of consumption and materialism.

Moreover, the decade saw a surge in speculative investment in the stock market. Many Americans, emboldened by the seemingly endless prosperity, poured their savings into stocks, hoping to capitalize on the booming market. The stock market became a symbol of wealth and success, with fortunes made seemingly overnight.

Factors Leading to the Stock Market Crash of 1929

Despite the apparent prosperity of the 1920s, underlying weaknesses in the economy began to emerge as the decade progressed. Several factors contributed to the eventual collapse of the stock market in 1929, leading to the onset of the Great Depression.

1. Overproduction and Underconsumption: The rapid expansion of industrial production during the 1920s led to an oversupply of goods, outpacing consumer demand. Despite rising wages and increased purchasing power for some segments of the population, many Americans could not afford the flood of new products saturating the market. This imbalance between production and consumption created a surplus of inventory, leading to declining prices and profit margins for businesses.

2. Unequal Distribution of Wealth: While the wealthy elite enjoyed unprecedented prosperity during the 1920s, the majority of Americans saw little improvement in their standard of living. Income inequality reached historic levels, with a small percentage of the population controlling the majority of the nation's wealth. The concentration of wealth in the hands of a few limited the purchasing power of the broader population, exacerbating the problem of underconsumption.

3. Speculative Stock Market Bubble: The stock market frenzy of the 1920s was fueled by speculative trading and excessive leverage. Many investors purchased stocks on margin, using borrowed money to amplify their potential gains. This speculative fever drove stock prices to unsustainable levels, detached from the underlying value of the companies they represented. As more investors joined the market in pursuit of quick profits, the stage was set for a dramatic reversal.

4. Weaknesses in the Banking System: The banking system of the 1920s was characterized by lax regulation and risky practices. Banks engaged in speculative investments and made loans to investors for stock market speculation. Additionally, many banks were undercapitalized and

vulnerable to runs by depositors seeking to withdraw their funds. The lack of effective oversight and safeguards left the banking system susceptible to collapse.

Overview of the Initial Impacts on American Society

The stock market crash of 1929 sent shockwaves throughout the American economy, triggering a chain reaction of events that reverberated across society. The immediate aftermath of the crash saw widespread panic and investor losses, as stock prices plummeted and fortunes evaporated overnight. In the days and weeks that followed, the full extent of the economic crisis became apparent as businesses shuttered, banks failed, and unemployment soared.

1. Economic Fallout: The collapse of the stock market precipitated a sharp decline in consumer spending and business investment, plunging the nation into a deep recession. Industries reliant on consumer demand, such as manufacturing and retail, were particularly hard hit, leading to widespread layoffs and factory closures. Unemployment skyrocketed, reaching double-digit levels in many parts of the country, as millions of Americans lost their jobs and struggled to make ends meet.

2. Banking Crisis: The stock market crash exposed weaknesses in the banking system, leading to a wave of bank failures and bank runs. Panicked depositors rushed to withdraw their savings, fearing the collapse of their banks. The failure of banks further exacerbated the economic downturn, as credit dried up and businesses struggled to obtain financing. The banking crisis deepened the sense of uncertainty and instability gripping the nation.

3. Social Dislocation: The economic upheaval of the Great Depression had profound social consequences, as families faced homelessness, hunger, and despair. Many Americans were forced to abandon their homes and migrate in search of work, leading to the rise of transient communities and shantytowns known as "Hoovervilles." Poverty and deprivation were widespread, with soup kitchens and breadlines becoming a common sight in cities across the country.

4. Psychological Impact: The Great Depression took a heavy toll on the mental and emotional well-being of millions of Americans. The loss of jobs, homes, and savings shattered the dreams and aspirations of countless individuals and families. Feelings of hopelessness, shame, and despair pervaded society, as people grappled with the uncertainty of their future. The psychological scars of the Great Depression would linger long after the economy began to recover.

Conclusion

The economic boom of the 1920s laid the foundation for the prosperity and excesses that would ultimately lead to the stock market crash of 1929. Despite the outward signs of wealth and progress, underlying weaknesses in the economy and financial system set the stage for a devastating economic downturn. The collapse of the stock market sent shockwaves throughout American society, triggering a cascade of events that would culminate in the Great Depression. The initial impacts of the crash were felt acutely by millions of Americans, as businesses failed, banks collapsed, and unemployment soared. The Roaring Twenties had come to a sudden and abrupt end, giving way to a decade of hardship and uncertainty.

Chapter 2: The Crash Heard Around the World

The stock market crash of 1929, often referred to as Black Tuesday, stands as one of the defining moments of the 20th century. Its impact reverberated far beyond Wall Street, sending shockwaves through the global economy and marking the beginning of the Great Depression. In this chapter, we will provide a detailed account of the events leading up to the crash, its immediate aftermath, the panic selling that ensued, the collapse of the financial markets, and the initial responses from government and business leaders.

The Buildup to Black Tuesday

The late 1920s saw a period of unprecedented speculation and exuberance in the stock market. Prices soared to dizzying heights as investors clamored to get in on the action, fueled by easy credit and the promise of quick riches. Companies were valued far beyond their intrinsic worth, with little regard for fundamentals such as earnings and dividends.

Throughout 1929, warning signs of an impending market correction began to emerge. The Federal Reserve, concerned about the speculative excesses in the market, began to tighten monetary policy by raising interest rates. This move, intended to curb speculation and prevent asset bubbles, had the unintended consequence of exacerbating the downturn.

In September 1929, cracks in the market's foundation began to widen. On September 3, the Dow Jones Industrial Average reached a peak of 381.17, signaling the culmination of the bull market. However, cracks in the market's foundation began to widen. On September 3, the Dow Jones Industrial Average reached a peak of 381.17, signaling the culmination of the bull market. However, cracks in the market's foundation began to appear, with several high-profile stocks experiencing sharp declines.

Despite these warning signs, many investors remained optimistic, convinced that the market would continue its upward trajectory indefinitely. Speculative fever reached a fever pitch in the weeks leading up to the crash, as investors borrowed heavily to finance their stock purchases, confident in the belief that prices would only continue to rise.

Black Tuesday: October 29, 1929

The morning of October 29 dawned like any other on Wall Street, but by the end of the day, the financial landscape of the United States would be forever altered. As trading began, nervous investors anxiously watched as stock prices began to plummet. Panic selling quickly ensued, as investors rushed to unload their shares before prices fell any further.

The frenzied selling triggered a chain reaction of margin calls and forced liquidations, further driving down prices and exacerbating the panic. By midday, the stock market was in free fall, with no end in sight. The ticker tape machines, which normally hummed with the steady rhythm of trading, churned out a relentless stream of red ink as stock prices tumbled.

As news of the crash spread, panic gripped the nation. Investors who had been riding high on the wave of prosperity suddenly found themselves facing ruin. Banks and brokerage firms, unable to meet the demands of panicked depositors and margin call holders, teetered on the brink of collapse.

By the end of the trading day, the Dow Jones Industrial Average had plummeted a staggering 38.33 points, or 12.82 percent, to close at 260.64. The losses were unprecedented, wiping out billions of dollars in wealth and decimating the portfolios of investors large and small.

The Immediate Aftermath

In the immediate aftermath of the crash, chaos reigned on Wall Street. The New York Stock Exchange was inundated with sell orders, overwhelming the floor traders and specialists tasked with executing trades. The trading floor descended into pandemonium as brokers shouted orders and frantically tried to match buyers with sellers.

Outside the stock exchange, crowds of onlookers gathered to witness the spectacle unfolding before them. Newsreel cameras captured the scenes of chaos, broadcasting them to audiences across the country and around the world. The crash had become a spectacle, a symbol of the excesses and follies of the Roaring Twenties.

As the dust began to settle, the full extent of the damage became apparent. The wealth of countless investors had been wiped out in a matter of hours, as stock prices plunged to levels not seen in years. Banks and brokerage firms faced imminent collapse, as depositors and margin call holders clamored to withdraw their funds.

Panic Selling and the Collapse of the Financial Markets

In the days and weeks following the crash, panic gripped the financial markets. Investors, fearful of further losses, continued to sell their stocks in droves, driving prices even lower. The selling pressure was relentless, with no respite in sight.

The collapse of the stock market had far-reaching consequences for the broader economy. Banks and brokerage firms, which had extended credit to investors for stock purchases, faced mounting losses as their clients defaulted on their loans. The banking system, already weakened by years of speculative excesses, teetered on the brink of collapse.

The panic spread beyond Wall Street, affecting businesses and consumers across the country. Confidence in the economy evaporated overnight, as consumers curtailed their spending and businesses scaled back their investment plans. Unemployment soared as companies laid off workers and shuttered their doors in the face of declining demand.

The collapse of the financial markets had profound social consequences as well. Families who had invested their life savings in the stock market saw their dreams of prosperity turn to dust. Retirees who had counted on their investments for income suddenly found themselves facing destitution. The human cost of the crash was immeasurable, as millions of Americans saw their hopes and aspirations dashed in an instant.

Initial Responses from Government and Business Leaders

In the wake of the crash, government and business leaders scrambled to contain the damage and restore confidence in the economy. President Herbert Hoover, who had been a staunch advocate of laissez-faire economics, initially downplayed the severity of the crisis, assuring the public that the fundamentals of the economy remained strong.

However, as the situation continued to deteriorate, Hoover was forced to take action. In November 1929, he convened a conference of business and banking leaders in an effort to coordinate a response to the crisis. The conference, which came to be known as the President's Conference on Unemployment, was intended to mobilize private sector resources to address the growing unemployment crisis.

Despite these efforts, the economy continued to spiral downward. Unemployment soared to levels not seen since the depths of the recession, as businesses slashed their payrolls in a desperate bid to cut costs. The banking system remained on the brink of collapse, as depositors continued to withdraw their funds in a panic.

In the face of mounting pressure, Hoover reluctantly turned to the federal government for assistance. In December 1929, he convened a special session of Congress to address the crisis, calling for measures to stimulate the economy and provide relief to those hardest hit by the downturn.

Conclusion

The stock market crash of 1929 was a seismic event that sent shockwaves through the global economy, marking the beginning of the Great Depression. The events of Black Tuesday, October 29, 1929, shattered the confidence of investors and triggered a panic that would reverberate for years to come. In the immediate aftermath of the crash, panic selling and the collapse of the financial markets wreaked havoc on the economy, leading to widespread unemployment, business failures, and social dislocation. Government and business leaders scrambled to contain the damage and restore confidence in the economy, but their efforts were largely ineffective. The crash of 1929 would go down in history as

a cautionary tale of the dangers of speculative excess and the perils of unchecked greed.

Chapter 3: Unraveling of the American Dream

The 1920s had been hailed as a decade of prosperity and opportunity, but the stock market crash of 1929 shattered the illusion of endless economic growth and brought the American Dream crashing down to earth. In this chapter, we will examine the unraveling of the American Dream in the wake of the Great Depression, focusing on the widespread unemployment and poverty that swept across the nation, the stories of families and individuals affected by job loss and homelessness, and the challenges faced by farmers and rural communities.

Widespread Unemployment and Poverty

The stock market crash of 1929 sent shockwaves through the American economy, triggering a devastating wave of unemployment and poverty. In the immediate aftermath of the crash, businesses across the country shuttered their doors, laying off workers and slashing payrolls in a desperate bid to cut costs. Unemployment soared to unprecedented levels, reaching double digits in many parts of the country.

For millions of Americans, the sudden loss of employment meant the loss of their livelihoods and the destruction of their hopes and dreams. Breadwinners who had once supported their families with steady jobs found themselves standing in breadlines, waiting for handouts to feed their hungry children. The specter of poverty loomed large, as families struggled to make ends meet on meager savings and dwindling assistance.

The impact of unemployment was felt acutely in urban areas, where industries such as manufacturing, construction, and retail were hit hardest by the downturn. Cities across the country became scenes of despair and destitution, as jobless workers flooded the streets in search of work and relief.

Stories of Families and Individuals Affected by Job Loss and Homelessness

Behind the statistics and economic indicators lay the human toll of the Great Depression. Countless families and individuals found themselves cast adrift in a sea of uncertainty, grappling with the harsh realities of unemployment and poverty.

In cities and towns across the country, families faced the heartbreaking prospect of homelessness as they were evicted from their homes and apartments for failing to make rent payments. Shantytowns and Hoovervilles sprung up on the outskirts of urban centers, populated by the newly homeless and destitute.

One such family was the Johnsons, who had once enjoyed a comfortable middle-class lifestyle in the suburbs of Chicago. When Mr. Johnson lost his job at the local factory after the crash, the family was forced to sell their home and move into a cramped apartment in the city. With no income and mounting debts, they struggled to put food on the table and keep a roof over their heads.

The plight of the Johnsons was echoed in communities across the country, as families who had once considered themselves secure and prosperous found themselves facing financial ruin. The American Dream of homeownership, upward mobility, and economic security seemed increasingly out of reach for millions of Americans.

Challenges Faced by Farmers and Rural Communities

While the Great Depression hit urban areas hardest, rural communities and farmers were not immune to its effects. In fact, many rural areas were already suffering from economic hardship long before the crash, as falling agricultural prices and mounting debts pushed farmers to the brink of bankruptcy.

The agricultural sector had been in decline throughout the 1920s, as overproduction and falling demand drove prices for crops such as wheat, corn, and cotton to historic lows. Farmers, already struggling to make ends meet, found themselves unable to repay their loans or cover their expenses, leading to widespread foreclosures and farm failures.

One such farmer was John Thompson, a tenant farmer in the Dust Bowl region of Oklahoma. Like many farmers in the area, John had borrowed heavily to finance his operations, hoping for a bountiful harvest that would allow him to repay his debts and provide for his family. But when the rains failed to come and the crops withered in the fields, John faced financial ruin.

The challenges facing farmers like John were compounded by the ecological disaster known as the Dust Bowl, which ravaged the Great Plains region throughout the 1930s. A combination of drought, overfarming, and poor land management practices led to the widespread erosion of topsoil, creating massive dust storms that engulfed the landscape and destroyed crops.

As farms failed and rural communities withered, thousands of families were forced to abandon their homes and migrate in search of work. Many headed westward, hoping to find employment in California's agricultural fields or in the booming industries of the Pacific Coast. But for most, the promise of a better life remained elusive, as jobs were scarce and competition fierce.

Conclusion

The unraveling of the American Dream during the Great Depression was a harrowing ordeal that touched the lives of millions of Americans from all walks of life. Widespread unemployment and poverty shattered the hopes and aspirations of countless families and individuals, casting them into a seemingly bottomless abyss of despair and destitution. Stories of families like the Johnsons and farmers like John Thompson serve as poignant reminders of the human cost of economic hardship and the enduring resilience of the American spirit. As the nation struggled to rebuild in the aftermath of the Great Depression, the lessons learned from this dark chapter in history would shape the course of American society for generations to come.

Chapter 4: Hoover's Response

As the Great Depression deepened and the economic crisis worsened, all eyes turned to President Herbert Hoover for leadership and solutions. In this chapter, we will delve into Hoover's response to the unfolding disaster, analyzing his policies and actions during the early years of the Depression. We will also examine the criticism of Hoover's approach, particularly his reliance on volunteerism, and the increasing public discontent and protests that marked his presidency.

Herbert Hoover's Rise to Power

Before we can understand Hoover's response to the Great Depression, it's essential to understand his background and rise to power. Herbert Hoover, a Republican and former Secretary of Commerce, was elected President in 1928 in a landslide victory over Democrat Alfred E. Smith. Hoover campaigned on a platform of continued prosperity and economic growth, promising to maintain the policies that had fueled the economic boom of the 1920s.

Hoover's reputation as a successful businessman and humanitarian had earned him widespread admiration and respect. He was hailed as the "Great Engineer" for his leadership in organizing relief efforts during World War I and his role in coordinating humanitarian aid to Europe in the aftermath of the war. Many Americans believed that his experience and expertise would serve him well in addressing the challenges facing the nation.

However, Hoover's presidency would be defined not by prosperity and progress but by the greatest economic crisis in American history.

Hoover's Policies and Actions During the Early Years of the Depression

When the stock market crashed in October 1929, Hoover initially downplayed the severity of the crisis, assuring the public that the fundamentals of the economy remained strong. He urged businesses to maintain wages and production levels, hoping to avoid widespread layoffs and economic disruption.

In the months following the crash, Hoover took several measures to address the economic downturn and provide relief to those affected by the crisis. He called on businesses to voluntarily maintain employment and wages, hoping to prevent mass layoffs and wage cuts. He also encouraged state and local governments to ramp up public works projects to create jobs and stimulate economic activity.

One of Hoover's most significant initiatives was the creation of the Reconstruction Finance Corporation (RFC) in 1932. The RFC was a government agency tasked with providing loans to banks, railroads, and other businesses to help stabilize the economy and prevent further collapses. While the RFC provided much-needed liquidity to struggling businesses, its efforts were largely ineffective in stemming the tide of bank failures and unemployment.

Despite these efforts, the economy continued to deteriorate, and public dissatisfaction with Hoover's response grew. By 1932, the unemployment rate had soared to over 20 percent, and millions of Americans were struggling to survive in the face of widespread poverty and deprivation.

Criticism of Hoover's Approach and the Failure of Volunteerism

One of the most significant criticisms of Hoover's response to the Great Depression was his reliance on volunteerism and private charity to address the crisis. Hoover believed that individual initiative and community efforts were sufficient to meet the needs of those affected by the downturn, and he resisted calls for direct government intervention in the economy.

Hoover's faith in volunteerism was evident in his creation of the President's Organization for Unemployment Relief (POUR) in 1930. POUR was a coalition of business leaders, community organizations, and philanthropic groups tasked with coordinating relief efforts and providing assistance to those in need. While POUR succeeded in mobilizing private resources and raising awareness of the plight of the unemployed, it was woefully inadequate in meeting the scale of the crisis.

The failure of volunteerism to address the economic crisis was painfully evident in the growing ranks of the unemployed and destitute. Breadlines and soup kitchens became a common sight in cities across the country, as millions of Americans struggled to feed their families and keep a roof over their heads. The gap between the rich and poor widened, as the wealthy elite continued to enjoy their privileged lifestyles while the masses suffered.

Increasing Public Discontent and Protests

As the Depression deepened and the suffering of the American people intensified, public discontent with Hoover's administration reached a boiling point. Hoover, once hailed as a hero and savior, was now seen as out of touch and indifferent to the plight of the common man.

Protests and demonstrations erupted across the country, as unemployed workers and disillusioned citizens took to the streets to demand relief and reform. In Washington, D.C., a group of World War I veterans known as the Bonus Army descended on the capital to demand early payment of bonuses promised to them for their service in the war. Hoover ordered the military to forcibly evict the veterans from their makeshift encampments, resulting in a violent clash that further tarnished his reputation.

The 1932 presidential election proved to be a referendum on Hoover's handling of the Depression, with Democrat Franklin D. Roosevelt soundly defeating him in a landslide victory. Hoover's presidency came to a close amidst widespread public disillusionment and despair, leaving behind a legacy of failed policies and broken promises.

Conclusion

Herbert Hoover's response to the Great Depression was marked by a combination of well-intentioned efforts and misguided policies. While Hoover deserves credit for his efforts to address the crisis and provide relief to those affected by the downturn, his reliance on volunteerism and reluctance to intervene directly in the economy proved to be his undoing.

As the Depression deepened and public discontent grew, Hoover's reputation as a capable and compassionate leader gave way to criticism and condemnation. His failure to stem the tide of unemployment and poverty, coupled with his heavy-handed response to protests and demonstrations, sealed his fate as one of the most reviled presidents in American history. Hoover's presidency serves as a cautionary tale of the dangers of ideological rigidity and the importance of proactive government intervention in times of crisis.

Chapter 5: The Dust Bowl Disaster

The Dust Bowl disaster of the 1930s stands as one of the most devastating ecological and agricultural catastrophes in American history. In this chapter, we will explore the ecological and agricultural factors that contributed to the Dust Bowl, the impact of the disaster on farmers in the Great Plains region, and the migration patterns of Dust Bowl refugees to California and other areas.

Explanation of the Ecological and Agricultural Factors Contributing to the Dust Bowl

The Dust Bowl was a man-made environmental disaster exacerbated by a combination of ecological and agricultural factors. The Great Plains region, which encompasses parts of Texas, Oklahoma, Kansas, Colorado, and New Mexico, experienced a period of rapid settlement and agricultural expansion in the late 19th and early 20th centuries. Homesteaders and farmers flocked to the region in search of land and opportunity, spurred by the promise of fertile soil and favorable climate.

However, the environmental conditions of the Great Plains were fragile and susceptible to degradation. The region's semi-arid climate, characterized by hot summers, cold winters, and erratic rainfall, made it prone to drought and erosion. The native grasses that once covered the plains had evolved to withstand these harsh conditions, forming a dense network of roots that held the soil in place and prevented erosion.

The arrival of European settlers and the mechanization of agriculture in the late 19th and early 20th centuries dramatically altered the landscape of the Great Plains. Large-scale farming operations replaced traditional methods of cultivation, as farmers cleared vast tracts of land for crops such as wheat, corn, and cotton. The native grasses, which had evolved to thrive in the harsh conditions of the plains, were replaced by shallow-rooted crops that offered little protection against erosion.

The introduction of mechanized farming equipment, such as tractors and plows, further exacerbated the problem by disrupting the delicate balance of the soil. Deep plowing and intensive cultivation practices exposed the soil to wind and water erosion, stripping away the protective cover of vegetation and leaving the land vulnerable to degradation.

The ecological impact of these agricultural practices was compounded by a series of severe droughts that struck the Great Plains region in the early 1930s. The combination of drought, high temperatures, and strong winds created ideal conditions for the formation of dust storms, which swept across the plains with devastating force, stripping away the topsoil and leaving behind a barren, desolate landscape.

Impact on Farmers in the Great Plains Region

The Dust Bowl had a catastrophic impact on the farmers and communities of the Great Plains region. Many farmers saw their livelihoods destroyed as their crops withered in the fields and their land turned to dust. The loss of income and productivity pushed thousands of families into poverty and destitution, as they struggled to feed themselves and their children.

Farmers who had once been prosperous and self-sufficient found themselves facing financial ruin and despair. The dust storms destroyed crops, killed livestock, and contaminated water supplies, leaving farmers with little means of support. Many were forced to abandon their land and migrate in search of work, leaving behind their homes and possessions in a desperate bid to survive.

The psychological toll of the Dust Bowl was immense, as farmers grappled with feelings of shame, failure, and hopelessness. The loss of their land and way of life shattered their dreams and aspirations, leaving them adrift in a sea of uncertainty and despair.

Migration Patterns of Dust Bowl Refugees to California and Other Areas

As the Dust Bowl worsened and the economic situation in the Great Plains deteriorated, thousands of farmers and their families began to migrate in search of work and relief. Many headed westward to California, lured by the promise of jobs in the agricultural fields and booming industries of the Pacific Coast.

The migration to California was fueled by a combination of desperation and hope, as families sought to escape the poverty and hardship of the Dust Bowl and build a better life for themselves and their children. However, the reality of life in California was often far from the idyllic image portrayed in popular culture.

Dust Bowl refugees, or "Okies" as they came to be known, faced discrimination and hostility from native Californians who viewed them as unwanted outsiders and competitors for jobs and resources. Many found themselves living in squalid migrant camps, where overcrowding, unsanitary conditions, and lack of access to basic amenities were commonplace.

Despite these challenges, many Dust Bowl refugees managed to carve out a new life for themselves in California, finding work in the agricultural fields, factories, and service industries of the state. Their resilience and determination in the face of adversity served as a testament to the human spirit and the enduring hope for a better future.

Conclusion

The Dust Bowl disaster of the 1930s was a testament to the fragility of the environment and the consequences of unsustainable agricultural practices. The ecological and agricultural factors that contributed to the Dust Bowl, combined with severe drought and economic hardship, created a perfect storm of devastation that upended the lives of thousands of farmers and their families in the Great Plains region.

The migration of Dust Bowl refugees to California and other areas was a desperate bid for survival and a testament to the resilience of the human spirit. Despite facing discrimination and hardship, many Dust Bowl refugees managed to rebuild their lives and find a new sense of hope and purpose in their adopted homes. The legacy of the Dust Bowl serves as a cautionary tale of the dangers of environmental degradation and the importance of sustainable land management practices in preserving the health and vitality of the land for future generations.

Chapter 6: Rise of the New Deal

The election of Franklin D. Roosevelt in 1932 marked a turning point in American history. With the nation mired in the depths of the Great Depression, Roosevelt's inauguration ushered in a new era of hope and optimism. In this chapter, we will explore Roosevelt's election and inauguration, the introduction of the New Deal programs aimed at providing relief, recovery, and reform, and the public response to Roosevelt's leadership as the beginning of hope for many Americans.

Overview of Franklin D. Roosevelt's Election and Inauguration

Franklin D. Roosevelt, a Democrat and former governor of New York, emerged as the standard-bearer of the Democratic Party in the 1932 presidential election. Running on a platform of bold reform and decisive action to address the economic crisis, Roosevelt promised a "New Deal" for the American people. His message of hope and optimism resonated with millions of voters who had grown disillusioned with the policies of President Herbert Hoover and the Republican Party.

The 1932 election proved to be a landslide victory for Roosevelt, as he defeated Hoover by a wide margin in both the popular vote and the Electoral College. On March 4, 1933, Roosevelt was inaugurated as the 32nd President of the United States, delivering a stirring inaugural address that would set the tone for his administration.

In his inaugural address, Roosevelt famously declared, "The only thing we have to fear is fear itself." His words struck a chord with a nation reeling from the effects of the Great Depression, offering a message of hope and reassurance in the face of adversity. Roosevelt pledged to take bold and decisive action to address the economic crisis and restore prosperity to the American people.

Introduction of the New Deal Programs

True to his word, Roosevelt wasted no time in implementing his agenda for change. In the first hundred days of his administration, Roosevelt and his advisers drafted and enacted a sweeping series of legislative measures known as the New Deal. The New Deal was a multifaceted program aimed at providing relief, recovery, and reform to address the economic crisis and put Americans back to work.

One of the cornerstones of the New Deal was the creation of the Civilian Conservation Corps (CCC), which provided employment to young men in conservation and public works projects. The CCC employed millions of young men across the country, planting trees, building trails, and restoring natural habitats. The program not only provided much-needed employment but also helped to preserve and protect the nation's natural resources for future generations.

Another key component of the New Deal was the establishment of the Works Progress Administration (WPA), which employed millions of Americans in a wide range of public works projects, including the construction of roads, bridges, schools, and parks. The WPA put millions of Americans back to work and helped to stimulate economic growth and recovery.

The New Deal also included a series of programs aimed at providing relief to those hardest hit by the Depression, including the Social Security Act, which established a system of old-age pensions and unemployment insurance, and the Federal Emergency Relief Administration (FERA), which provided direct assistance to the unemployed and needy.

Public Response to Roosevelt's Leadership

The introduction of the New Deal programs marked the beginning of a new era of hope and optimism for many Americans. Roosevelt's bold and decisive leadership inspired confidence and reassurance in a nation gripped by fear and uncertainty. The New Deal programs provided tangible relief to millions of Americans who had been struggling to make ends meet, offering a lifeline to those in need and a sense of hope for the future.

Public support for Roosevelt and his administration was overwhelming, as Americans rallied behind his efforts to address the economic crisis and restore prosperity to the nation. Roosevelt's popularity soared, and he was hailed as a hero and savior by millions of Americans who saw in him a beacon of hope in troubled times.

The public response to Roosevelt's leadership was not without its critics, however. Conservatives and business leaders accused Roosevelt of overreach and government interference in the economy, arguing that his New Deal programs were unconstitutional and infringed upon individual liberties. Others criticized Roosevelt for not going far enough in addressing the root causes of the Depression and for failing to enact more radical reforms.

Despite these criticisms, Roosevelt's leadership and the New Deal programs marked a turning point in American history. The New Deal reshaped the role of government in American society and laid the groundwork for the modern welfare state. Roosevelt's legacy as one of America's greatest presidents is indisputable, as his leadership during the Great Depression and World War II transformed the nation and inspired generations of Americans to believe in the power of government to improve their lives.

Chapter 7: Relief and Recovery Efforts

The Great Depression brought unprecedented hardship and suffering to millions of Americans, but it also spurred a wave of innovative and ambitious government programs aimed at providing relief and stimulating economic recovery. In this chapter, we will conduct a detailed examination of key New Deal programs such as the Civilian Conservation Corps (CCC), Public Works Administration (PWA), and Works Progress Administration (WPA). We will also explore the stories of individuals who benefited from these programs and assess the effectiveness of New Deal policies in alleviating hardship.

The Civilian Conservation Corps (CCC)

The Civilian Conservation Corps (CCC) was one of the most successful and popular New Deal programs, providing employment to millions of young men during the Great Depression. Established in 1933, the CCC was designed to address two pressing issues facing the nation: unemployment among young men and the conservation and development of the country's natural resources.

Under the leadership of the Army, the CCC recruited unemployed men between the ages of 18 and 25 to work on conservation and public works projects across the country. These projects included reforestation, soil conservation, flood control, and the construction of parks, trails, and recreational facilities.

The CCC provided participants with food, clothing, shelter, and a small wage, as well as education and vocational training opportunities. The program was immensely popular among young men who were eager to escape the economic hardship of the Depression and gain valuable skills and work experience.

One such individual was John Smith, a 20-year-old unemployed laborer from Alabama. Desperate for work and unable to find employment in his hometown, John joined the CCC in 1934 and was assigned to a reforestation project in the Appalachian Mountains. Over the next two years, John and his fellow CCC workers planted thousands of trees, built miles of hiking trails, and constructed recreational facilities for visitors to enjoy.

For John, the CCC provided not only a paycheck but also a sense of purpose and pride in his work. He gained valuable skills and experiences that would serve him well in his future career, and he formed lifelong friendships with his fellow CCC workers.

The Public Works Administration (PWA)

The Public Works Administration (PWA) was another key New Deal program aimed at stimulating economic recovery and creating jobs. Established in 1933, the PWA was responsible for funding and overseeing a wide range of public works projects, including the construction of roads, bridges, schools, hospitals, and other infrastructure.

The PWA employed millions of workers across the country, providing them with steady employment and a paycheck to support themselves and their families. The program was instrumental in revitalizing the nation's infrastructure and stimulating economic growth and recovery.

One notable example of a PWA project was the construction of the Hoover Dam on the Colorado River. Built between 1931 and 1936, the Hoover Dam was one of the largest and most ambitious public works projects of the New Deal era. The dam provided much-needed irrigation water and hydroelectric power to the arid Southwest, creating thousands of jobs and stimulating economic development in the region.

The Works Progress Administration (WPA)

The Works Progress Administration (WPA) was perhaps the most ambitious of all New Deal programs, employing millions of Americans in a wide range of public works projects and cultural programs. Established in 1935, the WPA was tasked with providing employment to unemployed workers and stimulating economic recovery through the construction of public infrastructure and the promotion of the arts and culture.

Under the leadership of Harry Hopkins, the WPA funded and oversaw a diverse array of projects, including the construction of roads, bridges, schools, and airports, the restoration of historic landmarks, and the creation of public murals, sculptures, and plays.

One of the most famous WPA projects was the Federal Art Project, which employed thousands of artists, writers, and performers to create works of art and literature that reflected the spirit of the times. Artists such as Jackson Pollock, Mark Rothko, and Willem de Kooning got their start in the WPA, producing some of their most iconic works during this period.

Assessment of the Effectiveness of New Deal Policies in Alleviating Hardship

The New Deal programs implemented by President Franklin D. Roosevelt were instrumental in providing relief and recovery to millions of Americans during the Great Depression. The CCC, PWA, and WPA, in particular, created millions of jobs and stimulated economic growth and recovery, lifting millions of Americans out of poverty and despair.

However, the effectiveness of New Deal policies in alleviating hardship varied widely depending on factors such as geography, race, and gender. African Americans and other minority groups faced discrimination and exclusion from many New Deal programs, limiting their access to employment and relief. Women, who were often relegated to low-paying and part-time jobs, also faced challenges in finding meaningful employment through New Deal programs.

Despite these limitations, the New Deal represented a bold and ambitious effort to address the economic crisis and provide relief to those hardest hit by the Great Depression. The programs implemented under the New Deal laid the groundwork for the modern welfare state and reshaped the role of government in American society. The legacy of the New Deal continues to resonate today, as Americans grapple with new challenges and seek solutions to address the pressing issues of our time.

Chapter 8: Challenges and Criticisms

While the New Deal brought hope and relief to millions of Americans during the Great Depression, it also faced significant challenges and criticisms from various quarters. In this chapter, we will conduct a detailed analysis of opposition to the New Deal from both the left and the right, criticisms of President Roosevelt's expansion of federal power and deficit spending, and the experiences of marginalized groups such as African Americans, women, and Native Americans during the Depression.

Opposition to the New Deal from Both the Left and the Right

The New Deal faced opposition from both ends of the political spectrum, with critics on the left and the right raising concerns about the effectiveness and fairness of Roosevelt's policies.

On the left, critics argued that the New Deal did not go far enough in addressing the root causes of the Depression and failed to adequately redistribute wealth and power in society. Socialist and communist groups, in particular, called for more radical measures such as nationalization of key industries and wealth redistribution through heavy taxation of the rich. They also criticized Roosevelt for his failure to address issues such as racial discrimination and economic inequality, which they saw as fundamental flaws in the capitalist system.

On the right, critics accused Roosevelt of overreach and government interference in the economy, arguing that his expansion of federal power threatened individual liberties and free-market principles. Conservative politicians and business leaders warned of the dangers of deficit spending and inflation, arguing that Roosevelt's policies would only prolong the Depression and saddle future generations with crippling debt.

Despite these criticisms, Roosevelt's popularity remained high among the American people, who saw in him a strong and decisive leader who was willing to take bold action to address the economic crisis.

Criticisms of Roosevelt's Expansion of Federal Power and Deficit Spending

One of the most common criticisms of the New Deal was Roosevelt's expansion of federal power and deficit spending to fund his programs. Critics argued that Roosevelt's policies represented a dangerous departure from traditional American values of limited government and fiscal responsibility, and warned of the long-term consequences of excessive government intervention in the economy.

Roosevelt's opponents pointed to the ballooning national debt and the growing size and scope of the federal government as evidence of his reckless spending and overreach. They argued that Roosevelt's policies were unsustainable and would ultimately lead to economic ruin and loss of individual freedom.

Critics also raised concerns about the constitutionality of many New Deal programs, arguing that Roosevelt had exceeded his authority as president and violated the principles of federalism enshrined in the Constitution. Several of Roosevelt's key initiatives, including the National Industrial Recovery Act (NIRA) and the Agricultural Adjustment Act (AAA), were challenged in court and ultimately struck down by the Supreme Court as unconstitutional.

Despite these criticisms, Roosevelt remained steadfast in his commitment to the New Deal and continued to push for further reforms to address the economic crisis and promote social justice.

Experiences of Marginalized Groups During the Depression

While the New Deal provided relief to millions of Americans, marginalized groups such as African Americans, women, and Native Americans faced unique challenges and obstacles during the Depression.

African Americans, who had long been marginalized and discriminated against in American society, faced widespread unemployment and poverty during the Depression. Many African Americans were excluded from New Deal programs and faced discrimination in hiring and relief efforts. The Works Progress

Administration (WPA), for example, employed far fewer African Americans than whites and often relegated them to low-paying and menial jobs.

Women also faced discrimination and exclusion from many New Deal programs, as relief efforts focused primarily on male breadwinners. Women were often relegated to low-paying and part-time jobs, and many struggled to support themselves and their families during the Depression. The Social Security Act, for example, initially excluded domestic and agricultural workers, who were disproportionately women and people of color, from eligibility for old-age pensions and unemployment insurance.

Native Americans, who had long been marginalized and oppressed by the federal government, also faced significant challenges during the Depression. Many Native American tribes were hit hard by the economic downturn and struggled to provide for their members. The Indian Reorganization Act of 1934, which sought to reverse decades of assimilationist policies and promote tribal self-government, was a step in the right direction, but it did not fully address the economic and social needs of Native American communities.

Conclusion

The New Deal was a bold and ambitious effort to address the economic crisis and provide relief to millions of Americans during the Great Depression. However, it also faced significant challenges and criticisms from both the left and the right, as well as from marginalized groups who felt excluded from its benefits.

Despite its flaws and shortcomings, the New Deal represented a watershed moment in American history, reshaping the role of government in society and laying the groundwork for the modern welfare state. The lessons learned from the New Deal continue to resonate today, as Americans grapple with new challenges and seek solutions to address the pressing issues of our time.

Chapter 9: Cultural Responses

The Great Depression was not just an economic crisis; it was a profound cultural and social upheaval that left an indelible mark on American society. In this chapter, we will explore how the arts, literature, and entertainment reflected the experiences of the Great Depression, highlighting notable works and artists of the period and examining the impact of the Depression on popular culture and societal values.

Exploration of How the Arts, Literature, and Entertainment Reflected the Experiences of the Great Depression

The Great Depression inspired a wave of artistic expression that captured the struggles, hardships, and resilience of the American people. From literature and visual arts to music and film, artists of all stripes sought to make sense of the chaos and uncertainty of the times and offer hope and solace to a nation in crisis.

In literature, the Great Depression gave rise to a new generation of writers who sought to capture the realities of life during the Depression with honesty and empathy. John Steinbeck's novel "The Grapes of Wrath," published in 1939, remains one of the most powerful and enduring literary works of the period, depicting the plight of Dust Bowl migrants as they struggle to survive and find a better life in California. Steinbeck's vivid prose and sympathetic portrayal of the Joad family struck a chord with readers and critics alike, earning him the Pulitzer Prize for Fiction and solidifying his reputation as one of America's greatest writers.

In visual arts, the Great Depression inspired a wave of social realism and documentary photography that sought to capture the struggles and resilience of ordinary Americans. Artists such as Dorothea Lange, Walker Evans, and Gordon Parks produced iconic images that remain seared in the collective memory of the nation, documenting the faces and stories of the Depression with compassion and insight.

In music, the Great Depression gave rise to a new genre of protest songs and folk ballads that spoke to the experiences of the downtrodden and dispossessed. Artists such as Woody Guthrie, Lead Belly, and Pete Seeger used music as a tool for social commentary and political activism, singing about the struggles of working-class Americans and the need for social justice and reform.

In film, the Great Depression inspired a new era of realism and social consciousness in Hollywood, as filmmakers sought to address the pressing issues of the day with honesty and integrity. Classic films such as "Gone with the Wind," "The Wizard of Oz," and "Mr. Smith Goes to Washington" reflected the hopes, fears, and aspirations of Americans during the Depression, offering escapism and inspiration in equal measure.

Notable Works and Artists of the Period

The Great Depression produced a wealth of notable works and artists across a wide range of artistic disciplines, each offering a unique perspective on the times and the human condition.

One of the most iconic images of the Great Depression is Dorothea Lange's photograph "Migrant Mother," taken in 1936 during the height of the Dust Bowl migration. The photograph, which depicts a destitute mother and her children huddled together in a makeshift shelter, has become a symbol of the hardships faced by ordinary Americans during the Depression and a testament to the power of photography to evoke empathy and understanding.

John Steinbeck's novel "The Grapes of Wrath" remains one of the most enduring literary works of the Great Depression, offering a searing indictment of the social and economic injustices of the time. The novel's vivid portrayal of the Joad family's journey from the Dust Bowl to California struck a chord with readers and critics alike, earning Steinbeck the Pulitzer Prize for Fiction and cementing his reputation as one of America's greatest writers.

In music, Woody Guthrie's folk ballads and protest songs captured the spirit of the Great Depression with raw honesty and passion. Songs such as "This Land Is Your Land," "Deportee," and "Hard Travelin'" spoke to the struggles of ordinary Americans and the need for social justice and solidarity.

In film, Frank Capra's "Mr. Smith Goes to Washington" remains a classic of the era, offering a stirring portrayal of one man's fight against corruption and injustice in the halls of power. The film's message of hope and idealism struck a chord with audiences during the Depression, offering a much-needed reminder of the power of the individual to effect change in society.

Impact of the Depression on Popular Culture and Societal Values

The Great Depression had a profound impact on popular culture and societal values, shaping the way Americans thought about themselves and their place in the world.

The hardships of the Depression fostered a spirit of resilience and solidarity among Americans, as communities came together to support one another in the face of adversity. The "Dust Bowl Ballads" of Woody Guthrie and the "Okie" novels of John Steinbeck celebrated the strength and resilience of ordinary Americans in the face of overwhelming odds, offering a message of hope and solidarity in troubled times.

At the same time, the Depression exposed the fault lines and inequalities of American society, highlighting the stark divides between rich and poor, black and white, urban and rural. The social realist photography of Dorothea Lange and Walker Evans captured the faces and stories of the forgotten men and women of the Depression, shining a spotlight on the struggles of the marginalized and dispossessed.

The cultural responses to the Great Depression reflected a growing awareness of the need for social justice and reform in American society. Artists, writers, and musicians used their talents to raise awareness of the issues facing the nation and to advocate for change, inspiring a new generation of activists and reformers to take up the cause of social justice and equality.

Conclusion

The Great Depression was a time of profound upheaval and change in American society, as the nation grappled with the economic crisis and its social and cultural ramifications. The arts, literature, and entertainment of the period offered a window into the experiences of ordinary Americans and a reflection of the values and aspirations of the nation.

From the social realism of Dorothea Lange and John Steinbeck to the protest songs of Woody Guthrie and the idealism of Frank Capra's films, the cultural responses to the Great Depression continue to resonate with audiences today, offering a timeless reminder of the resilience and spirit of the American people in the face of adversity.

Chapter 10: The Second New Deal

As the Great Depression continued to grip the nation in its icy grasp, President Franklin D. Roosevelt launched a series of additional New Deal programs aimed at addressing the deep-rooted economic and social challenges facing the country. In this chapter, we will delve into the Second New Deal, which introduced landmark legislation such as Social Security, the Wagner Act, and the Fair Labor Standards Act. We will focus on the efforts to address labor rights and social welfare, as well as the debate over the effectiveness and long-term consequences of these policies.

Introduction of Additional New Deal Programs

The Second New Deal, launched in 1935, represented a continuation and expansion of President Roosevelt's efforts to combat the economic crisis and provide relief to millions of Americans. Building on the foundations laid by the First New Deal, the Second New Deal introduced a series of sweeping reforms aimed at addressing labor rights, social welfare, and economic inequality.

One of the most significant achievements of the Second New Deal was the passage of the Social Security Act in 1935. The Social Security Act established a system of old-age pensions, unemployment insurance, and welfare benefits for the elderly, disabled, and unemployed. The program provided a safety net for millions of Americans who were struggling to make ends meet during the Great Depression, offering them a measure of security and dignity in their old age.

Another key piece of legislation introduced during the Second New Deal was the Wagner Act, also known as the National Labor Relations Act, which was passed in 1935. The Wagner Act guaranteed workers the right to organize and bargain collectively with their employers, and established the National Labor Relations Board (NLRB) to enforce labor laws and resolve disputes between workers and management. The Wagner Act marked a significant victory for the labor movement and helped to empower workers to demand fair wages, better working conditions, and greater job security.

The Fair Labor Standards Act, passed in 1938, was another important piece of legislation introduced during the Second New Deal. The Fair Labor Standards Act established a national minimum wage, limited the number of hours that could be worked in a week, and prohibited child labor in certain industries. The law represented a major step forward in the fight for workers' rights and helped to improve the lives of millions of Americans who were struggling to make ends meet.

Focus on Efforts to Address Labor Rights and Social Welfare

The Second New Deal was characterized by a renewed focus on efforts to address labor rights and social welfare, as President Roosevelt sought to build on the successes of the First New Deal and expand the reach of government intervention in the economy.

The passage of the Wagner Act was a major victory for the labor movement and helped to strengthen the bargaining power of workers in industries such as manufacturing, transportation, and mining. The establishment of the National Labor Relations Board (NLRB) provided workers with a forum to air their grievances and seek redress for unfair labor practices, and helped to level the playing field between labor and management.

The Social Security Act was another landmark achievement of the Second New Deal, providing a safety net for millions of Americans who were struggling to make ends meet during the Great Depression. The Social Security program offered a measure of security and dignity to the elderly, disabled, and unemployed, and helped to alleviate poverty and hardship among the most vulnerable members of society.

The Fair Labor Standards Act, meanwhile, helped to establish basic standards of fairness and decency in the workplace, setting a national minimum wage and limiting the number of hours that could be worked in a week. The law represented a significant victory for workers' rights and helped to improve the lives of millions of Americans who were struggling to make ends meet.

Debate over the Effectiveness and Long-Term Consequences of These Policies

Despite the successes of the Second New Deal in addressing labor rights and social welfare, the policies introduced during this period were not without controversy, and sparked a fierce debate over their effectiveness and long-term consequences.

Critics of the Second New Deal argued that Roosevelt's expansion of federal power and intervention in the economy threatened individual liberties and free-market principles, and warned of the dangers of deficit spending and inflation. Conservative politicians and business leaders accused Roosevelt of overreach and government interference in the economy, and argued that his policies would only prolong the Depression and saddle future generations with crippling debt.

Others raised concerns about the sustainability of the Social Security program and the long-term solvency of the Social Security Trust Fund. Skeptics questioned whether the government would be able to fulfill its promises to future generations of retirees, and warned of the need for reforms to ensure the program's viability in the years to come.

Despite these criticisms, the Second New Deal represented a bold and ambitious effort to address the economic crisis and provide relief to millions of Americans during the Great Depression. The policies introduced during this period laid the groundwork for the modern welfare state and reshaped the role of government in American society, leaving a lasting legacy that continues to resonate today.

Chapter 11: Shifting Tides of Hope

As the 1930s drew to a close, the United States found itself on the cusp of a new era, marked by shifting tides of hope and optimism after years of economic hardship and social upheaval. In this chapter, we will examine signs of economic recovery and improvement in the late 1930s, the impact of World War II on American industry and employment, and the lasting legacy of the Great Depression in shaping government policy and public attitudes.

Examination of Signs of Economic Recovery and Improvement in the Late 1930s

By the late 1930s, the United States began to see signs of economic recovery and improvement after years of depression and stagnation. While the road to recovery was long and arduous, several key factors contributed to the gradual turnaround in the nation's fortunes.

One of the most significant developments was the expansion of government intervention in the economy through programs such as the New Deal. President Franklin D. Roosevelt's policies aimed at stimulating economic activity and providing relief to those hardest hit by the Depression began to bear fruit, as government spending helped to create jobs and stimulate demand for goods and services.

The Second New Deal, introduced in the mid-1930s, introduced additional reforms aimed at addressing labor rights and social welfare, such as the Social Security Act and the Fair Labor Standards Act. These programs provided a safety net for millions of Americans who were struggling to make ends meet, offering them a measure of security and dignity in their old age.

Another factor contributing to the economic recovery was the growing confidence and optimism among consumers and businesses. As the nation began to emerge from the depths of the Depression, consumer spending and business investment began to pick up, helping to fuel economic growth and create new opportunities for employment and prosperity.

The impact of these developments was felt across the country, as communities began to see signs of revitalization and renewal after years of hardship and despair. New industries began to emerge, driven by technological innovation and changing consumer preferences, while traditional industries such as manufacturing and agriculture experienced a resurgence in demand.

Impact of World War II on American Industry and Employment

The outbreak of World War II in Europe in 1939 marked a turning point in American history, as the United States began to mobilize for war and ramp up its production capacity to support the Allied war effort. The war had a profound impact on American industry and employment, transforming the nation into the "Arsenal of Democracy" and laying the groundwork for postwar economic prosperity.

As the demand for military equipment and supplies skyrocketed, American factories shifted into high gear, churning out tanks, planes, ships, and munitions at an unprecedented rate. The war effort created millions of new jobs in industries such as manufacturing, construction, and transportation, providing employment to millions of Americans who had been struggling to find work during the Depression.

The influx of federal spending also helped to stimulate economic growth and fuel consumer demand, as workers earned higher wages and had more money to spend on goods and services. The war effort brought millions of women and minorities into the workforce for the first time, as they took on jobs traditionally held by men who had gone off to fight overseas.

The impact of World War II on American industry and employment was profound and far-reaching, laying the foundation for postwar economic expansion and prosperity. The war effort not only helped to lift the nation out of the Great Depression but also transformed the United States into a global superpower and set the stage for the economic dominance that would define the latter half of the 20th century.

Legacy of the Great Depression in Shaping Government Policy and Public Attitudes

The Great Depression left a lasting legacy in shaping government policy and public attitudes, as policymakers and the American people grappled with the lessons learned from the economic crisis and its aftermath.

One of the most significant legacies of the Great Depression was the expansion of government intervention in the economy through programs such as the New Deal. President Franklin D. Roosevelt's bold and ambitious efforts to combat the economic crisis and provide relief to millions of Americans laid the groundwork for the modern welfare state, reshaping the role of government in American society and paving the way for future reforms.

The New Deal programs introduced during the Great Depression helped to establish a social safety net for the most vulnerable members of society, providing unemployment insurance, old-age pensions, and welfare benefits to those in need. These programs represented a fundamental shift in the way Americans thought about the role of government in addressing social and economic issues, and set the stage for future efforts to promote social justice and equality.

The legacy of the Great Depression also had a profound impact on public attitudes toward government and the economy. The economic hardships and social upheaval of the Depression fostered a growing sense of distrust and disillusionment with traditional institutions and authorities, as many Americans felt abandoned and betrayed by the political and economic elites who had failed to prevent the crisis.

As a result, there was a growing demand for greater government intervention in the economy and society, as people looked to the federal government to provide relief and support in times of need. The New Deal coalition, which brought together a diverse array of interest groups and constituencies in support of Roosevelt's policies, reflected this growing consensus for government action to address social and economic issues.

Conclusion

The Great Depression was a defining moment in American history, leaving an indelible mark on the nation's economy, society, and culture. The economic hardships and social upheaval of the Depression fostered a sense of resilience and solidarity among Americans, as communities came together to support one another in the face of adversity.

As the nation emerged from the depths of the Depression, signs of economic recovery and improvement began to emerge, fueled by government intervention and the growing confidence and optimism of consumers and businesses. The outbreak of World War II marked a turning point in American history, as the United States mobilized for war and transformed itself into the "Arsenal of Democracy," laying the groundwork for postwar economic prosperity and global leadership.

The legacy of the Great Depression continues to resonate today, as policymakers and the American people grapple with the lessons learned from the economic crisis and its aftermath. The expansion of government intervention in the economy and society, the social safety net established during the New Deal, and the enduring demand for greater government action to address social and economic issues all reflect the lasting impact of the Great Depression on American society and governance.

Chapter 12: Lessons Learned

The Great Depression stands as one of the most defining and tumultuous periods in American history, leaving a profound impact on the nation's economy, society, and politics. In this chapter, we will reflect on the causes and consequences of the Great Depression, assess the role of government in responding to economic crises, and analyze how the Depression reshaped American society and politics.

Reflection on the Causes and Consequences of the Great Depression

The Great Depression was triggered by a complex set of factors, including the stock market crash of 1929, widespread bank failures, and a sharp decline in consumer spending and investment. The collapse of the stock market sent shockwaves through the economy, leading to a cascade of business failures, layoffs, and bankruptcies.

As businesses shuttered their doors and workers lost their jobs, consumer demand plummeted, exacerbating the economic downturn and plunging the nation into a downward spiral of deflation and depression. The agricultural sector was particularly hard hit, as falling crop prices and drought conditions in the Midwest led to widespread farm foreclosures and rural poverty.

The consequences of the Great Depression were devastating, with millions of Americans losing their jobs, homes, and savings. Families were forced to stand in breadlines and soup kitchens, while shantytowns known as "Hoovervilles" sprang up in cities across the country. The psychological toll of the Depression was equally profound, as people struggled to cope with the stress and uncertainty of living in a world turned upside down.

Assessment of the Role of Government in Responding to Economic Crises

The Great Depression challenged traditional notions of the role of government in the economy, as policymakers grappled with how best to respond to the crisis and provide relief to those hardest hit by the downturn. President Franklin D. Roosevelt's New Deal represented a bold and ambitious effort to combat the economic crisis and promote social welfare through government intervention and public works programs.

The New Deal introduced a wide range of reforms aimed at addressing the root causes of the Depression and providing relief to those in need. Government agencies such as the Works Progress Administration (WPA), the Civilian Conservation Corps (CCC), and the Social Security Administration (SSA) provided employment, relief, and social insurance to millions of Americans, helping to stabilize the economy and restore confidence in the government.

The New Deal also represented a fundamental shift in the way Americans thought about the role of government in society, as people looked to the federal government to provide leadership and support in times of crisis. The expansion of government intervention in the economy and society laid the groundwork for the modern welfare state, reshaping the relationship between the state and its citizens and establishing a framework for future efforts to promote social justice and economic opportunity.

Analysis of How the Depression Reshaped American Society and Politics

The Great Depression had a profound and lasting impact on American society and politics, reshaping the way people thought about themselves, their government, and their place in the world. The economic hardships and social upheaval of the Depression fostered a sense of resilience and solidarity among Americans, as communities came together to support one another in the face of adversity.

The New Deal coalition, which brought together a diverse array of interest groups and constituencies in support of Roosevelt's policies, reflected this growing consensus for government action to address social and economic issues. The legacy of the New Deal continues to resonate today, as Americans grapple with new challenges and seek solutions to address the pressing issues of our time.

The Great Depression also had a profound impact on American politics, as the crisis exposed the fault lines and inequalities of American society and fueled calls for radical change. The rise of populist and socialist movements, as well as the emergence of figures such as Huey Long and Father Charles Coughlin, reflected the growing dissatisfaction with the status quo and the desire for greater government intervention in the economy and society.

Conclusion

The Great Depression was a watershed moment in American history, leaving an indelible mark on the nation's economy, society, and politics. The causes and consequences of the Depression continue to be studied and debated by scholars and policymakers, as we seek to learn from the mistakes of the past and build a better future for generations to come.

The lessons learned from the Great Depression are as relevant today as they were in the 1930s, as we confront new challenges and seek solutions to address the pressing issues of our time. By reflecting on the causes and consequences of the Depression, assessing the role of government in responding to economic crises, and analyzing how the Depression reshaped American society and politics, we can gain valuable insights into how to build a more resilient, equitable, and prosperous future for all Americans.

Chapter 13: Remembering the Great Depression

The Great Depression remains etched in the collective memory of American society as a time of immense hardship, resilience, and social upheaval. In this chapter, we will examine how the Great Depression is remembered and commemorated in American culture, explore the legacy of the Depression era in family histories and personal narratives, and discuss the continued relevance of the lessons of the Depression in contemporary society.

Examination of How the Great Depression is Remembered and Commemorated in American Culture

The Great Depression holds a prominent place in American cultural memory, with numerous books, films, songs, and artworks dedicated to capturing the experiences of those who lived through the era. From iconic photographs of breadlines and Hoovervilles to classic films such as "The Grapes of Wrath" and "It's a Wonderful Life," the Depression has been immortalized in popular culture as a time of struggle, sacrifice, and resilience.

One of the most enduring images of the Great Depression is Dorothea Lange's photograph "Migrant Mother," which depicts a destitute mother and her children huddled together in a makeshift shelter. The photograph has become a symbol of the hardships faced by ordinary Americans during the Depression and a testament to the power of photography to evoke empathy and understanding.

Literature has also played a key role in shaping our understanding of the Great Depression, with authors such as John Steinbeck, Richard Wright, and Studs Terkel offering vivid portrayals of life during the era. Steinbeck's novel "The Grapes of Wrath," in particular, remains one of the most powerful and enduring literary works of the period, depicting the plight of Dust Bowl migrants as they struggle to survive and find a better life in California.

In addition to literature and visual arts, music has also played a significant role in commemorating the Great Depression, with artists such as Woody Guthrie, Lead Belly, and Billie Holiday using their music to capture the spirit of the times and advocate for social justice and reform. Songs such as "This Land Is Your Land," "Strange Fruit," and "Goodnight Irene" remain powerful reminders of the struggles and triumphs of the era.

Legacy of the Depression Era in Family Histories and Personal Narratives

The legacy of the Great Depression lives on in the family histories and personal narratives of those who lived through the era, as memories of hardship and resilience are passed down from generation to generation. For many families, the Depression represents a defining moment in their history, shaping the way they think about themselves and their place in the world.

Personal narratives of the Depression era often focus on stories of struggle, sacrifice, and survival, as families grappled with unemployment, poverty, and uncertainty. Many people who lived through the era recount tales of making do with what they had, stretching every penny, and relying on the kindness of friends and neighbors to get by.

At the same time, the Depression era is also remembered as a time of solidarity and community, as people came together to support one another in the face of adversity. Stories of mutual aid, shared sacrifice, and collective action abound in the personal narratives of those who lived through the era, serving as a testament to the resilience and strength of the human spirit.

Continued Relevance of the Lessons of the Depression in Contemporary Society

Despite the passage of time, the lessons of the Great Depression remain as relevant today as they were in the 1930s, as we confront new challenges and seek solutions to address the pressing issues of our time. The economic hardships and social upheaval of the Depression serve as a stark reminder of the dangers of unchecked greed and speculation, as well as the importance of strong social safety nets and government intervention in times of crisis.

In an era marked by growing income inequality, stagnant wages, and economic insecurity, the lessons of the Depression serve as a cautionary tale against the dangers of unchecked corporate power and financial speculation. The collapse of the housing market in 2008 and the subsequent global financial crisis were stark reminders of the risks of deregulation and lax oversight, as well as the need for strong government intervention to prevent economic collapse and protect the most vulnerable members of society.

The COVID-19 pandemic, which has exposed and exacerbated existing inequalities and vulnerabilities in our society, has also underscored the importance of the lessons of the Depression era. As millions of Americans struggle to make ends meet in the face of job losses, evictions, and food insecurity, the need for robust social safety nets and government intervention to support those in need has never been clearer.

Conclusion

The Great Depression remains a defining moment in American history, leaving an indelible mark on the nation's culture, society, and politics. From iconic photographs and literary works to personal narratives and family histories, the Depression continues to shape the way we think about ourselves and our place in the world.

As we reflect on the legacy of the Great Depression, we are reminded of the resilience and strength of the human spirit in the face of adversity. The lessons of the Depression serve as a timeless reminder of the dangers of unchecked greed and speculation, as well as the importance of strong social safety nets and government intervention in times of crisis. By remembering and commemorating the experiences of those who lived through the era, we honor their sacrifices and ensure that the lessons of the Depression are never forgotten.

Chapter 14: Enduring Resilience

The Great Depression was a time of unprecedented economic hardship and social upheaval in American history. However, amidst the challenges and adversity, stories of resilience and perseverance emerged, showcasing the indomitable human spirit. In this chapter, we will explore these stories of resilience, examining how individuals and communities coped with hardship and found sources of hope, and discuss the enduring legacy of resilience in American culture and identity.

Stories of Resilience and Perseverance During the Great Depression

The Great Depression brought about immense suffering and uncertainty for millions of Americans, but it also gave rise to countless stories of resilience and perseverance. Despite facing daunting challenges, individuals and communities across the country demonstrated remarkable resilience in the face of adversity.

One such story is that of the WPA (Works Progress Administration) workers who, through federally funded projects, built roads, bridges, schools, and parks across the nation. These projects not only provided much-needed employment for millions of Americans but also left a lasting legacy of public infrastructure that continues to benefit communities to this day.

Another example of resilience during the Great Depression is the establishment of community-led initiatives such as soup kitchens, breadlines, and homeless shelters. In cities and towns across the country, ordinary citizens came together to provide food, shelter, and support to those in need, demonstrating the power of collective action in times of crisis.

Individuals also demonstrated resilience in their personal lives, finding creative ways to make ends meet and provide for their families despite the economic hardships. From planting victory gardens to sewing clothes and mending shoes, people found innovative ways to stretch their limited resources and weather the storm of the Depression.

Examination of How Individuals and Communities Coped with Hardship and Found Sources of Hope

During the Great Depression, individuals and communities coped with hardship in a variety of ways, drawing on their resilience, resourcefulness, and sense of solidarity to navigate the challenges they faced.

For many, faith and spirituality provided a source of comfort and solace in times of uncertainty. Churches, synagogues, and mosques served as centers of community and support, offering spiritual guidance, emotional support, and material assistance to those in need.

Others found solace in the simple pleasures of family, friends, and community. Despite the economic hardships, people found joy in spending time with loved ones, sharing meals, and celebrating holidays and milestones together.

Creativity and self-expression also played a key role in helping individuals cope with the hardships of the Depression. Whether through art, music, literature, or storytelling, people found ways to express themselves and find meaning in their experiences, fostering a sense of hope and resilience in the face of adversity.

Legacy of Resilience in American Culture and Identity

The legacy of resilience forged during the Great Depression continues to resonate in American culture and identity, shaping the way we think about ourselves and our place in the world.

One enduring legacy of the Depression era is the belief in the power of community and collective action to overcome adversity. The spirit of solidarity and mutual aid that emerged during the Depression laid the groundwork for future social movements and grassroots initiatives aimed at promoting social justice and equality.

The resilience of the American people during the Great Depression also serves as a reminder of the importance of perseverance and determination in the face of hardship. The stories of individuals and communities who endured unimaginable suffering and adversity, yet refused to give up hope, inspire us to keep pushing forward in the face of our own challenges and setbacks.

Moreover, the legacy of resilience forged during the Great Depression continues to inform our understanding of American identity, shaping the way we think about ourselves and our values as a nation. The belief in the power of the individual to overcome adversity and build a better future for themselves and their community remains a central tenet of the American dream, inspiring generations of Americans to strive for a better tomorrow.

Conclusion

The Great Depression was a time of immense hardship and suffering for millions of Americans, but it was also a time of resilience, solidarity, and hope. Despite facing daunting challenges, individuals and communities across the country demonstrated remarkable resilience in the face of adversity, finding creative ways to cope with hardship and build a brighter future for themselves and their loved ones.

The legacy of resilience forged during the Great Depression continues to resonate in American culture and identity, reminding us of the enduring strength and resilience of the American people. As we confront new challenges and uncertainties in the years ahead, we can draw inspiration from the stories of those who lived through the Depression, finding hope and strength in their example as we work to build a better, more resilient future for all.

Chapter 15: Looking to the Future

As we reflect on the enduring impact of the Great Depression on American society and economics, we are reminded of the lessons learned and the challenges still faced in ensuring economic security and social welfare for all Americans. In this chapter, we will explore the lasting legacy of the Great Depression, consider the lessons learned from this tumultuous period in history, and issue a call to action for building a more equitable and resilient future for all.

Reflection on the Enduring Impact of the Great Depression on American Society and Economics

The Great Depression left an indelible mark on American society and economics, reshaping the way we think about ourselves, our government, and our economy. The economic hardships and social upheaval of the Depression laid bare the vulnerabilities and inequalities of American society, exposing the flaws and shortcomings of the laissez-faire approach to economic governance.

One of the enduring legacies of the Great Depression is the recognition of the need for strong social safety nets and government intervention in the economy to protect the most vulnerable members of society. The New Deal programs introduced during the Depression laid the groundwork for the modern welfare state, providing unemployment insurance, old-age pensions, and welfare benefits to those in need.

The Depression also sparked a fundamental shift in the way Americans thought about the role of government in society, as people looked to the federal government to provide leadership and support in times of crisis. The expansion of government intervention in the economy and society laid the foundation for future efforts to promote social justice and economic opportunity.

Consideration of Lessons Learned and Challenges Still Faced

Despite the progress made since the Great Depression, significant challenges remain in ensuring economic security and social welfare for all

Americans. Income inequality, stagnant wages, and rising costs of living continue to threaten the economic stability and well-being of millions of Americans, particularly those from marginalized and underserved communities.

The COVID-19 pandemic has exposed and exacerbated existing inequalities and vulnerabilities in our society, highlighting the need for robust social safety nets and government intervention to support those in need. The pandemic has disproportionately impacted low-income workers, people of color, and other marginalized groups, exacerbating existing disparities in access to healthcare, education, and economic opportunity.

Moreover, the climate crisis presents another existential threat to the well-being and prosperity of future generations. The impacts of climate change, including extreme weather events, rising sea levels, and diminishing natural resources, threaten to exacerbate existing inequalities and disrupt economies around the world.

Call to Action for Building a More Equitable and Resilient Future for All Americans

As we look to the future, it is incumbent upon us to heed the lessons of the Great Depression and work towards building a more equitable and resilient society for all Americans. This requires a concerted effort to address the root causes of economic inequality and social injustice, and to ensure that all Americans have access to the resources and opportunities they need to thrive.

Investing in education, healthcare, and affordable housing is essential to promoting economic mobility and opportunity for all Americans. Additionally, strengthening labor rights and protections, raising the minimum wage, and ensuring access to affordable healthcare and childcare are critical steps towards building a more inclusive and equitable economy.

Furthermore, addressing the climate crisis requires bold and ambitious action to transition to a sustainable and resilient economy.

Investing in clean energy, sustainable infrastructure, and green jobs will not only help to mitigate the impacts of climate change but also create new opportunities for economic growth and prosperity.

Conclusion

The Great Depression remains a powerful reminder of the importance of resilience, solidarity, and collective action in times of crisis. As we reflect on the enduring impact of the Great Depression on American society and economics, we must consider the lessons learned and the challenges still faced in ensuring economic security and social welfare for all Americans.

By investing in education, healthcare, and affordable housing, strengthening labor rights and protections, and addressing the climate crisis, we can build a more equitable and resilient future for all Americans. It is incumbent upon us to heed the lessons of the past and work towards building a society that promotes opportunity, justice, and prosperity for all. Together, we can create a brighter future for ourselves and future generations.

Don't miss out!

Visit the website below and you can sign up to receive emails whenever Michael Johnson publishes a new book. There's no charge and no obligation.

https://books2read.com/r/B-A-OREFB-APKAD

Connecting independent readers to independent writers.

Did you love *The Great Depression*? Then you should read *The Cold War*[1] by Michael Johnson!

[2]

Explore the riveting saga of the Cold War, from its tumultuous beginnings to its epochal conclusion. Unveil the geopolitical chessboard of post-World War II as the United States and the Soviet Union ascend as superpowers, igniting tensions that reverberate worldwide. From the Truman Doctrine to the Cuban Missile Crisis, McCarthyism to the Vietnam War, delve into the ideological battlegrounds and proxy conflicts that defined an era. Witness the thaw of détente and the seismic shifts of perestroika, culminating in the historic collapse of the Soviet Union. Experience the legacy and lessons of this epochal standoff, resonating into the 21st century.

---

1. https://books2read.com/u/3L8985

2. https://books2read.com/u/3L8985

About the Author

Michael Johnson is a distinguished historian specializing in American history. With a degree in History from Harvard University, Johnson's work delves into pivotal moments, figures, and themes shaping the United States. He has authored numerous acclaimed books, offering insightful perspectives and engaging narratives. Johnson's commitment to meticulous scholarship and compelling storytelling has earned him widespread acclaim in the field. Passionate about sharing his expertise, he frequently engages in lectures and public events to foster a deeper appreciation for America's past.